THE 15
MOST AMAZING
PSYCHOLOGICAL EXPERIMENTS

… and what they revealed about
human nature

THE 15
MOST AMAZING
PSYCHOLOGICAL EXPERIMENTS

... and what they revealed about
human nature

RICARDO CALZA GONZÁLEZ

CreateSpace Independent Publishing Platform
1st edition (March 2016); v22

ISBN-13: 978-1530317349
ISBN-10: 1530317347

Ψ

"They are vain and are riddled with errors sciences unborn from the experiment, mother of all certainty."
Leonardo Da Vinci

"Human being is an experiment; time will show whether it was worth."
Mark Twain

ÍNDICE

DEAR READER...

With this first page begins the book that will tell you some of the most famous and amazing experiments conducted in the field of psychology, and which are the lessons to be drawn on the way human mind works.

Psychology is a very young science. Its birth dates back to 1879, when Wilhelm Wundt, considered as the father of modern psychology, founded the first laboratory for investigating the basis of human consciousness, at the University of Leipzig (Germany).

This date is considered the birth of psychological science because in his research Wundt was in line with the principles of scientific method.

Basically, scientific method says that to understand a phenomenon an experiment should be designed to discover why and how it occurs, and also says that to be considered valid, the findings of an experiment must be reproducible at any time and place.

Through his experiments, Wundt investigated the role perceptions, sensations, feelings, will and attention play in shaping people's consciousness.

It's because this 'youth' of psychology that the reader will find that most of the experiments reported here were carried out during the twentieth century, when all of the different theoretical schools in psychology became eager to know more about the human psychological processes.

This does not mean psychological experiments are no longer performed, but I decided to choose these fifteen experiments because, due to the still relatively brief history of psychology as a science, the time has passed since they were made and their impact and influence on the understanding of human mind, today all of them are considered as 'classic'.

Any scientific experiment, no matter what field of knowledge it belongs, may seem, at first, limited, because at its early stages cannot be guessed what impact or consequences the secrets it reveals can have on the daily lives of people.

Thus, it is very likely someone watching footages of the first experiments carried out by rocket engineers during the earliest decades of the twentieth century, only observes a group of people in a field with a kind of big toy that rises a few meters above the ground only to end crashing down moments later.

At that time, very few observers could have realized these were the precursors of a series of scientific advances allowing missiles to travel from one continent to another or rockets to take man to the moon.

Due to the rigor of scientific method, when a researcher describes his experiment, he or she must explain whether or not the initial hypothesis is supported by the results of the experiment. Their conclusions must be adjusted, carefully and methodically, to be consistent with the results. No one is allowed to speculate about the influence the results of an experiment may have on future applications and researches, at least not on the scientific paper.

But the truth is that experiments, often carried out in university basements and small laboratories, with limited resources, using students as collaborators or as experimental subjects, sometimes exceed initial expectations and become significant discoveries, developments and inventions, influencing the lives of many people, and in some cases, even the very course of human history.

This can also happen with experiments in psychology. Sometimes, their performances are even more surprising than those from experiments made in other fields of science, because to explore human nature many of them put people in situations that easily awaken interest and curiosity.

I recommend to the reader, when reflecting on them, do not dwell only on the empirical findings their authors describe, but also let the imagination fly to consider the implications any of these investigations can have on a broader level, explaining human nature.

Understanding human psyche allows us to better predict people's behavior, either in a particular circumstance, throughout our own lives, a psychological illness or disorder, a social event or even history itself.

The ethics of the experiments

For the title of this book I could have used, instead of *amazing*, many other adjectives, because to the reader, and to myself, some of the experiments here narrated will seem curious, some shocking, some cruel and others perplexing, among many other possible reactions. However, several of the investigations here described share a common qualifier: influential. Some of them have brought a revolution to the science of human psychology and changed completely the idea people had at the time they were made on the way human mind worked.

But contrary to what Oscar Wilde said in the prologue of his book The Picture of Dorian Grey, about art "*is not moral or immoral*," scientific experiments can be ethical or unethical, depending on whether they are adjusted to a certain code of research conduct and respect for the rights of people and animals. Unfortunately, as the reader will see, this has not always been the case. Obviously, I reject the design and the way some of the studies described here were performed.

Human nature is complex and none of us are free from making serious mistakes, even if we pursue a goal we consider good or positive. Furthermore, at the time some of the studies were carried out ethical standards for scientific research had not yet been developed. Even some of them contributed, indirectly, in establishing limits for what could or could not be done in a scientific investigation. In some cases, years later even the authors themselves were sorry for what they had done in their experiments.

However, it's not my intention to judge neither the experiments nor its authors, but just present them to the readers and expose how they contributed to explain how people feel, think and behave. Let everyone draw their own conclusions about the ethical or not of each investigation.

Divulgative intention

My intention is to describe and explain the experiments to contribute to the divulgation of psychology. I intend to transmit the idea that psychology is a science, and as such, its study and application does not respond to insights, philosophies or wisdoms.

To facilitate this divulgative intention, I will not go deep on technical, methodological discussions or details about the results of each investigation, all of these issues should be restricted to scientific and academic fields, and must be treated by more knowledgeable and prepared professionals than me.

Thus, the book's goal is to transmit scientific knowledge as well as be entertaining, fun, easy to read and contribute to the divulgation and popularization of psychology as a science.

I do not intend at any time to replace the original works of the authors, but only give some general notions of every research to thereby stimulate interest and respect for scientific knowledge. I refer to the original works for all those who want to know more clearly and better about the experiments here described.

At the end of each chapter, in the *References* section, the original scientific paper related to the experiment discussed is cited; it has been my main reference for the elaboration of the chapter. At the *Documentary sources* section, I have cited other resources that have been useful to gather the information of each investigation.

A personal experience

Although the title of the book says here you will find fifteen experiments, in fact they are sixteen, because as the last experiment I have taken the liberty of sharing with you a personal experience, which occurred when I was a young university student and decided to volunteer on a psychological research performed for one of my teachers.

Something happened in the course of that experiment has been with me for years, and as much as I have tried to rid myself of it, I have failed.

Who knows, maybe even to decide writing this book is nothing more than an unconscious way of reckoning with what happened that day… but on second thought, I do not think so. I do not think subconscious has so much power over behavior.

"MONSTER STUDY": THE MONSTROUS EXPERIMENT

The experiment later known as the "Monster Study" has the scholarly title of *An Experimental Study of the Effect of Evaluative Labeling of Speech Fluency*. This is the name of a doctoral thesis in which an experiment was conducted to investigate the causes of stuttering.

It was designed in 1939 by Wendell Johnson, a psychologist and professor at the University of Iowa, and implemented by Mary Tudor, a student working on her doctoral thesis under the direction of Professor Johnson.

The experiment was carried out with orphaned children belonging to the Soldiers and Sailors Orphans Home of Davenport (Iowa, US) and lasted five months, from January to May of 1939. The intention of the experiment was to purposely induce stuttering in some children using 'psychological pressure.'

More than 200 children were evaluated for the experiment, of which 22 were finally chosen, with ages ranging from 5 to 16 years; 10 of them had problems of stuttering while 12 did not show any difficulty when speaking. The children were divided into two groups: those who stuttered and those who did not. Then each group was divided in two, the experimental group and the control group.

The experiment consisted of positive reinforcement, using praises, the verbal execution of children belonging to the control groups. The experimenter maintained conversations with them in the room where the study was being conducted and downplayed any fault or error committed by them when speaking, encouraging the children to work towards correcting it and telling them they would be able to overcome it.

Meanwhile, the verbal performance of children of the experimental group was negatively reinforced, constantly drawing their attention to any fault committed and telling them they were stutterers or would become one if they continued making that mistake (for example, a doubt, a pause or a casual repetition of a syllable or word during the conversation, caused a child to be told he could turn into a stutterer, provoking him or her a considerable amount of anxiety and insecurity).

In both cases, the orphanage staff was instructed to continue positive or negative reinforcement, according to which group each child belonged, outside the experimental sessions.

Results

To the researchers, the results obtained at the end of the experiment showed that the type of reinforcement used (positive or negative) influenced the occurrence, development or improvement of speech problems and disorders, what supported the theory of Professor Johnson about stuttering is not innate but learned, and that this alteration of speech has psychological causes, based on negative reactions to faults and normal speech problems.

Negative reactions to corrections or negative comments from parents or other people could cause a child to develop anxiety due to a minor mistake made when talking, a mistake that would had disappeared over time if he or she had not been reprimanded.

The evidence obtained with these results would be very useful in designing treatments for this disorder.

However, once the experiment was over, several of the children who had been verbally punished suffered permanent psychological damages because of the emotional impact of the psychological pressure received. This made some of them carry speech problems for the rest of their lives (unfortunately, the orphanage staff continued to administer the verbal reinforcement after the end of the experiment).

A broader and liberal interpretation of the results could be how to strengthen or reprimand can influence people, even causing them psychological damages, later manifested in the most basic behaviors, which may persist for a long time, causing very serious alterations and problems over the course of their lives.

The nickname

When some of Professor Johnson's colleagues heard of the experiment, they were horrified, and referred to it as the "Monster Study."

The Professor, fearful of how the experiment could affect his career (considering news was beginning to arrive regarding Nazi experiments on humans at that time), decided not to publicize the results in any scientific journal. To this day, only Mary Tudor's thesis is preserved as written evidence of the experiment.

The responsible

Professor Wendell Johnson knew very well the suffering that stuttering can cause. He himself was a stutterer and for years had suffered shame, insecurity, limitations and most likely, humiliation.

During his student days he volunteered in all kinds of experiments, in order to investigate this speech disorder. He devoted his entire career to the understanding of stuttering, occupying several academic and professional positions relating to the research and treatment of this speech pathology.

In view of his biography, it does not seem unreasonable to assume his affliction had made an impact on the right perspective for the ethics of his experiment.

Mary Tudor declared, on interviews granted years later, that at the time the experiment was conducted she often felt depressed when seeing how it affected the children's speech. She tried to justify the research by proclaiming the results obtained had been useful in helping many people overcome stuttering.

Years later she received letters from former participants in the experiment, calling her a "monster" and accusing her of ruining their lives.

In 2001 the University of Iowa (where Wendell Johnson was a professor) publicly apologized for the experiment, and in 2007 several participants received financial compensation from Iowa State for damages caused by the experiment which went down in the history of psychology by the name of the Monster Study.

References

Ambrose, N. G. & Yairi, E. (2002). *The Tudor Study: Data and Ethics.* American Journal of Speech-Language Pathology. Vol 11, pp. 190–203. doi: 10.1044/1058-0360(2002/018)

Tudor, M. (1939). *An Experimental Study of the Effect of Evaluative Labeling of Speech Fluency*. Iowa: University of Iowa.

DOCUMENTARY SOURCES

BBC News (August 17, 2007). *Huge payout in US stuttering case.* London: BBC. Recovered from http://news.bbc.co.uk/ 2/hi/americas/6952446.stm

Dyer, J. (June 10, 2001). *Ethics and Orphans: The `Monster Study'.* San Jose Mercury News, The Mercury News. Recovered from http://www-psych.stanford.edu/~bigopp/stutter2. html

Dyer, J. (June 7, 2001). *An experiment leaves a lifetime of anguish.* San Jose Mercury News, The Mercury News. Recovered from http://www.uiowa.edu/~cyberlaw/hsr /wj-sjmn/orphan061101-2.htm

Johnson, N. (1999). *Wendell A. L. Johnson (1906-1965). Memorial Home Page.* Iowa, IA: Nicholas Johnson. Recovered from http://www.nicholasjohnson.org/ wjohnson

MILGRAM EXPERIMENT: BLIND OBEDIENCE TO AUTHORITY

The experiment known as Milgram Experiment was actually a series of experiments, made between 1961 and 1962. The researcher's goal was to find out why people tend to obey the orders of authority, even when those orders are considered bad or unfair, and go against some basic personal principles.

The author

Stanley Milgram (1933-1984) was an American psychologist who specialized in social psychology. Originally a graduate in Political Science, he obtained a doctorate in Social Psychology from Harvard University Center, where he worked as an associate professor, as well as at Yale University, where he conducted his famous experiment.

During his years as a university student, Milgram demonstrated leadership skills in his relationships with peers. Perhaps it was this ability, along with his abhorrence of the Holocaust of World War II, in which eleven million people were murdered, which led him to investigate the psychological mechanisms within human beings which make them to obey orders unquestionably.

His research showed people tend to obey orders coming from those they perceive as authority even when they disagree with those orders.

This was demonstrated by the fact that up to 65% of the study participants complied with the orders they were given to continue administering severe electric shocks to someone, even when he or she complained about the enormous suffering they produced.

We will now look at how the most representative of this series of experiments was conducted.

The experiment

A newspaper advertisement asked volunteers to be part of an experiment at Yale University for which they would be paid $4 for one hour of work.

From all of the people who responded, only 40 were finally selected, aged between 20 and 50 years, from different occupations and social level.

The participants were told the object of the experiment was to demonstrate the effect punishment had on the learning capacity and memory (as I said before, which was really intended was to see if there was a psychological explanation for obedience). The researchers made it clear the money would be earned for merely participating, and was not depended on what was done during the experiment.

The participants should ask a series of questions to a person, in order to test the human capacity to learn and memorize. If the answers were wrong, they should give to the subject an electric shock.

The electric discharges were administered by a machine, having 30 different levels of intensity. Discharges ranged from 15 to 450 Volts, and were designated as *light, moderate, strong, very strong, intense, very intense, dangerous* and *XXX*.

With this classification, participants would have a clear idea of the pain they could cause (over 195 Volts an electric discharge was marked as very strong). The fact that people receiving discharges emitted groans, lamentations and cries as intensity increased also helped to make participants aware of the pain they inflicted.

But what the participants were unaware was people answering questions (called *victims*) were in fact accomplices of the experiment. Electrical discharges did not really reach them and the pain expressed was entirely faked.

As the victim committed errors when answering, the experimenter ordered the participants to increase the discharge voltage, giving them one of four types of orders depending on the level of resistance to deliver discharges they showed:

1.– Please continue.
2.– The experiment requires that you continue.
3.– It is absolutely essential that you continue.
4.– There is no alternative, you must go on.

Because of the increasingly intense 'discharges' at each stage the victim pretended to endure greater suffering, pleading to stop the experiment. To make it more credible, the victim was strapped down to a chair, so the participant thought all the control over the situation depended on him.

Results

All of the 40 participants in the experiment obeyed the orders and continued to administer the discharges even when the voltage was greater than 280 Volts (rated as *very intense*).

Between that level and the penultimate (435 Volts, rated as more than severe, XXX) 14 participants refused orders to continue, and at the last discharge level (450 Volts), the remaining 26 refused to follow the orders of the experimenter.

This means that 100% of participants continued to obey orders when the discharge was already described as very intense and the victim gave clear signs of suffering. 65% of them reached the penultimate level, where the discharge was considered dangerous. Although all of them showed increasing signs of stress and nervousness caused by the orders received, they tended to continue obeying.

Interpretation

The results show to what extent humans have some psychological mechanisms making us tend to obey authority.

These mechanisms probably have a social origin, because throughout a person's education, constantly the notions of authority and obedience are inculcated, either from family, school, work or social life, in many different ways.

The results of this experiment were taken as proof that people tend to follow the orders of those considered a legitimate authority, in who we delegate the power to make decisions, especially in confusing or stressful situations. As a result of this attitude, humans are obedient to orders or instructions we receive, even if we are aware those orders are immoral or will cause some kind of harm to others.

Of course, there are limits, as it was shown by the fact none of the participants agreed to administer the maximum discharge. But it is quite possible they all went much farther than they thought they would, which is a clear demonstration of the human trend to obey authority figures.

References

Milgram, S. (1963). *Behavioral Study of Obedience*. Journal of Abnormal and Social Psychology. Vol 67, No 4, pp. 371-378. doi: 10.1037/h0040525.

DOCUMENTARY SOURCES

Blass, T. (2007). *Stanleymilgram.com*. Baltimore, MD: Thomas Blass. Consulted on http://www.stanleymilgram.com

Milgram, S. (2004*). Obedience to Authority: An Experimental View*. New York: HarperCollins.

THE STANFORD PRISON EXPERIMENT: CAUSES AND EFFECTS OF EVIL

The intention of this classic experiment was to investigate the psychological effects that playing the role of guard or prisoner has on people.

The study was commissioned by the Office of Naval Research of the United States Navy, who wanted to know the causes of conflicts and riots in military prisons. It was conducted in August 1971 by a team of researchers led by Philip Zimbardo, a psychologist and professor at Stanford University.

The experiment aimed to find out how people's behavior changes as a result of being in the role of prisoner or guard in a prison.

The study was designed to last two weeks, during which the participants played the role of either guards or prisoners. But the effects of putting people in this situation turned out to be so dramatic that it had to be stopped after just six days. Considering what happened during the first few days of the experiment, one can only imagine the very serious events which might have happened if the experiment had been allowed to continue.

Recruitment

During a quiet summer morning in August 1971, in the city of Palo Alto, Santa Clara County, California (US) a police raid took place in which 24 men were arrested, on charges of theft and armed robbery. Curiously, all the detainees are university students.

But this is not what it seemed. The 24 'arrested' men had been chosen from among 70 candidates who had volunteered to participate in the experiment that went down in history as the Stanford Prison Experiment.

And so, in this rather spectacular and realistic way, the experiment began. Taken out from their homes, participants were detained and handcuffed by real cops, who read them their rights in the same way they would have done with real criminals. After getting into police cars, they were all taken to the police station.

Once there, they were identified, going so far as even to take their fingerprints. After the arrest process was completed, they were locked in a cell to await their next destination.

No doubt many were already having second thoughts about volunteering for this experiment, during this waiting period. Maybe the $15 a day for their participation no longer seemed like easy money. But they had signed an agreement and there was no going back.

The prison

Once this first part was over, they were moved to the 'prison.' Nine of the twenty four participants were designated to play the role of prisoners and nine to play guards. The remaining six would be in reserve.

The prison was actually constructed in the basement of Stanford University's Department of Psychology, in accordance with advice from a real ex-prisoner with sixteen years of 'experience.'

The old laboratories were transformed into cells and the hall became the prison yard. There was even an isolation cell, along with several toilets. It had no windows or clocks, to cause spatial and temporal disorientation in the 'inmates.' Cameras and microphones were placed strategically to record every detail of the experiment.

After arriving, participants playing the role of prisoners were undressed and disinfected. They had become real prisoners and the true experiment had begun.

In order to humiliate them, prisoners were given a poor uniform (a sack to cover them) with a serial number by which they would be called from then on. They were not provided underwear and were forced to wear a chain around the ankle. A kind of cap was used to simulate their heads having been shaved.

The participants who played guards did not receive such poor treatment. On the contrary, they were given full freedom. They were never instructed on how to behave or what rules the prisoners were to follow. They themselves decided what rules should prevail in prison. To facilitate their role play, they received a uniform, a whistle, a truncheon and sunglasses.

It was no long before the guards began to exercise their power. They forced prisoners to do push-ups as punishment, and on the first night inmates were awoken in the middle of the night for a head count. The consequences of this abuse of power soon appeared, and during the second morning the prisoners rebelled against the guards with a riot.

After the first moments of confusion, the guards reacted violently against the prisoners' insults and disobedience (they had locked the cells doors using beds as barricades) using fire extinguishers to keep prisoners away from doors and into their cells. And this was only the second day of the experiment.

With the rebellion repressed, the guards increased the humiliations, preferring psychological over physical punishment. A privilege cell was prepared for inmates with good behavior and thus inmates were divided into *good* and *bad*. All inmates had to relieve themselves in buckets without allowing them to remove the buckets from the cells once full.

On the third day an inmate suffered the first case of nervous breakdown. *"It was a real prison (...). I felt completely hopeless,"* said prisoner number 8612 during a later interview. He was excused from participating in the experiment and was allowed to leave the prison.

On the fourth day a strict regime of visits was established, only permitting contact with families for ten minutes each visit.

But it seemed prisoner 8612, out of the prison because the emotional crisis he had suffered, did not want to leave behind his prison mates. After over hearing some conversations between prisoners, the guards uncovered the rumor 8612 was planning to attack the prison, free his comrades and end the cruel experiment.

In the end this was just a rumor and 8612 did not attack the prison. But this showed how a situation could quickly become more complicated and revealed a possible cause of prison riots.

As the experiment continued the guards delved deeper into their role and the humiliations increased. Meanwhile, the inmates increasingly accepted their role by becoming more obedient and submissive to the guards' cruel treatment.

One of the prisoners declared himself on hunger strike. Guards, sadistically, gave to other inmates the opportunity to save him from solitary confinement if they would all give up their blankets. Most of them preferred their fellow inmate to be held in solitary confinement. Dehumanization was spreading quickly between guards and prisoners.

As the experiment progressed, prisoners began to suffer depersonalization, nervous crises and other psychological disturbances. A group of parents, concerned about what their children had told them during visits, and from reports from a priest who had been visiting the 'prison', requested Professor Zimbardo to immediately release their children.

Everything had become too real: abuse of power, riots, rumors, punishments and parents demanding the release of their children... At this point, Zimbardo decided to end the experiment.

In August 20, only six days after the experiment began, all participants were allowed to leave the prison where they had spent a few days they would not forget for the rest of their lives.

Conclusions

This study shows how easily conflicts emerge between people when certain kind of power relations exists between them.

People in charge in this kind of situations can too easily, if not controlled, establish abusive rules to suppress and obliterate the personalities of those under their power.

Among those who suffer power abuse a considerable amount of frustration and feelings of hatred and revenge appears, remaining long after the events, as shows what one of the former 'inmates' said in an interview a few months after the end of the experiment: *"I only think about killing those who have beaten me and treated like a dog."*

All the attitudes, behaviors and feelings observed in the experiment can become part of a dangerous mix within a prison situation, which can lead to all sorts of situations, from complaints, protests, hunger strikes or aggressions, to the outbreak of violent riots.

In a broader interpretation, the Stanford Prison Experiment should be used to reflect on human nature, and which mechanisms, both individual and collective, we must establish to prevent trends and most basic instincts to control our behavior, making us exceed ethical limits and personal values.

Do not forget that all participants, just before starting the experiment, were young people, middle-class college students, defined as healthy and intelligent by aptitude tests. It only took a few hours in a situation like the one designed for the experiment, to reveal behaviors and attitudes that are, at least, surprising, saddening and disturbing.

Curiosities

Professor Zimbardo himself acknowledged that during those six days he sometimes thought more like a prison warden, worried more about maintaining *status quo* than a researcher conducting an experiment.

The six days at the Stanford prison were extensively documented. At the website Professor Zimbardo dedicated to the experiment anyone can access some of the research photos and videos, including interviews with the participants (see link to website in *References*).

In 2001 the German film *Das Experiment*, directed by Oliver Hirschbiege, was released. It was inspired by the book *Black Box*, from author Mario Giordano, which was based on the Stanford Prison Experiment.

References

Zimbardo, P. G. (1999-2014). *Stanford Prison Experiment*. San Francisco, CA: Philip G. Zimbardo. Consulted on http://www.prisonexp.org

DOCUMENTARY SOURCES

Conrad, M., Evenkamp, P., Herrmann, B., Leibfried, U., Preuss, N. & Wildfeuer, F. (produces) & Hirschbiegel, O. (director) (2001). *Das experiment (The experiment)*. [Movie film]. Germany: Typhoon (as Typhoon Film), Fanes Film, Senator Film Produktion (with), Seven Pictures (in co-production with) (as SevenPictures).

Giordano, M. (2001*). Das experiment- Black Box*. Reinbek: Rowohlt.

Zimbardo, P. G. (2008). *El efecto Lucifer. El porqué de la maldad*. Barcelona: Paidós Ibérica.

PAVLOV'S DOG EXPERIMENT: THE POWER OF CONDITIONING

This is probably the most famous experiment in the field of psychology, although far from being the most surprising, shocking, spectacular or most entertaining.

In my opinion, the most important point about this experiment is the implications of its results. But despite being arguably the most famous psychological experiment, paradoxically it was not carried out by a psychologist, but a physician.

Pavlov

Ivan Petrovich Pavlov (1849-1936) was a Russian physiologist, professor of Physiology at the Imperial Medical Academy and director of the Department of Physiology of the Institute of Experimental Medicine in St. Petersburg (Russia).

He focused his professional work on investigating the functioning of the digestive system. His studies led him to be awarded the Nobel Prize for Physiology or Medicine in 1904.

And in his quest to understand the digestive tract, between 1890 and 1900 he designed and performed a simple experiment which demonstrated what became known as *Classical Conditioning*.

The experiment

Professor Pavlov was trying to find out what causes the body to salivate in the presence of food. For this, he designed a simple but effective experiment in which he used a dog as experimental subject.

The experiment consisted of four phases:

The first phase was to confirm the dog salivated when presented with food.

During the second phase a sound was made to the dog (a bell or buzzer). This was to check there was no salivation reaction to this stimulus.

In the third phase, the dog was shown food several times after hearing the sounds used in the second phase.

In the fourth phase only the sound was made to the dog. At this last phase, Pavlov saw the animal reacted by salivating. This occurred because the dog had come to associate the sound with food presentation. The animal *learned* that the sound preceded the food, and that learning was so strong the body reacted with the same response as if the food was present. Therefore, the physiological response (salivation) had a psychological origin.

The results showed that the association of a stimulus that caused a specific subject's response with a neutral one could cause the same response as the first. During the experiment, the dog learned the sound was the condition for food to appear. So, the sound became what Pavlov called a *conditioned stimulus*.

With this experiment, Pavlov proved the existence of physiological conditioned responses, i.e., through experience the body can learn to develop reflex responses to stimuli which on their own would not trigger any reaction.

Consequences

I consider this experiment as one of the most amazing in psychology because of the implications it has on our daily lives.

Imagine for a minute the importance conditional associations may have on influencing people. Almost all publicity is based, in some way, on creating associations between a neutral stimulus to us (e.g. a car, a detergent or a drink) with another that causes a reflex reaction, so we end up associating both and thus being conditioned.

This would explain why cars are often associated with beautiful models, perfumes with the concepts of elegance or social acceptance, or politicians with positive images (the image of a politician kissing a child). And this is not only true in a positive sense: conditioning people in order to associate fear, uncertainty and insecurity with something or someone, can be used to distort their view of reality.

On an individual level, it is not difficult to deduce that conditioning is behind memories, sensations, feelings and even psychological disorders such as phobias (mental disorders in which a person develops a pathological fear to a certain type of stimulus, due to some traumatic past event).

Do not think you are free of this process just because you know of it. The conditioning occurs automatically because it is based on repetition, it is not a conscious process over which you have any control. It causes us to associate a stimulus previously neutral to us with an uncontrollable physiological response.

The conditioning is so powerful that it has even been found in simple cell organisms such as amoebas.

It has been a long time since I first learned of classical conditioning while studying psychology as a college student. I clearly remember the impact it had on me as I listened to the lecturer. That day, when reviewing my notes, I became aware of how my reactions, understanding of life and will could be conditioned if suitable mechanisms were used.

A long time has passed since then, but I still find it easy to re-awake the feeling that evoked in me when I first learned of Pavlov's Dog Experiment.

Curiosities

When this experiment is discussed people always talk of "Pavlov's dog," but actually several animals were used in the course of his investigations, although history recognizes all of them as if they were just one, the famous Pavlov's dog. At the house-museum in honor of the physiologist in his hometown, Ryazan, one can still see one of the dissected canine specimens used in his experiments

When psychology was first developed in the United States during the early twentieth century, a theoretical movement known as *Behaviorism* emerged. This approach had a great importance on psychology and influenced much of the later theoretical and practical development of this science. Behaviorism had among its fundamental bases the classical conditioning discovered by Pavlov, over which many theoretical explanations were developed. Some behaviorists even thought they could create practical interventions to influence the behavior of people, to the point they could change almost every aspect of human psychology and behavior at will.

References

Pavlov, I. P. (1927). *Conditioned Reflexes: An Investigation of the Physiological Activity of the Cerebral Cortex*. London: Oxford University Press. Consulted on http://psychclassics.yorku.ca/Pavlov

DOCUMENTARY SOURCES

Alcaraz García, M. A., Redondo Lago, J. M., Fraga Carou, I. and Fernández-Rey, J. (2003). *Procesos psicológicos básicos I.* Madrid: Ediciones Pirámide.

Nobelprize.org. (2013). *Nobelprize.org. The Official Web Site of the Nobel Prize.* Stockholm, Sweden: Nobel Media AB. Consulted on http://www.nobelprize.org/nobel_prizes/medicine/ laureates/1904

Pavlov, I. P. (2010). *Conditioned Reflexes: An Investigation of the Physiological Activity of the Cerebral Cortex.* Annals of Neurosciences, Vol 17, No 3. doi: 10.5214/ans.0972-7531.1017309

LITTLE ALBERT EXPERIMENT: "BRING ME A HEALTHY CHILD AND HE WILL BECOME WHOEVER I WANT"

The Little Albert Experiment was designed and carried out by the famous psychologist John B. Watson and one of his students, Rosalie Rayner, at the Johns Hopkins University. The results were published in 1920 in the Journal of Experimental Psychology.

The author

John Broadus Watson (1878-1958) was the principal founder of the movement known as Behaviorism, one of the most important approaches in modern psychology.

One of the Behaviorism's theoretical foundations is classical conditioning, discovered by the Russian physiologist Ivan Petrovich Pavlov in 1890-1900. This principle revealed a stimulus A could, through the appropriate mechanisms, be associated with a stimulus B, so that A, by itself, ended up causing the same reaction as B (see *Pavlov's Dog Experiment* chapter).

During the experiment in which this principle was first demonstrated, Pavlov caused dogs to salivate at the mere presence of a sound, by making them associate the sound with the presence of food.

John B. Watson went far beyond. Fervently convinced of the nearly limitless power of classical conditioning, he rejected the weight of genetics on human behavior. For him only the environment determined how animals and humans behave and react. He was so convinced of this he said if someone entrusted him with the education of a child chosen at random, he could make the child become the kind of adult he decided, by using only the behaviorism principles of behavior modification, including classical conditioning, with the only condition that the child fulfilled some minimum health requirements.

And so, he set about his claim on a little boy referred to as Albert for the experiment, along with his assistant, a graduate student, Rosalie Rayner.

The Little Albert and the experiment

Albert B. was a child of about nine months old, son of a Johns Hopkins University employee (where Watson and Rayner would conduct the experiment) and a nurse.

The objective of the research was to accomplish the conditioning on Albert, an emotionally healthy child, so that he would eventually develop fear of an animal (a white mouse) to which he was previously shown feel no fear at all.

The experiment was quite simple. First, it was confirmed Albert felt no fear in the presence of a white mouse, or animals or objects with similar characteristics. To do this, the child was exposed to the presence of a white rat, a rabbit, a dog, a monkey, a mask with feathers, woolens or newspapers, while Watson checked Albert for any negative reactions to any of these stimuli.

After confirming the absence of fear to these animals and objects, Albert was exposed to a very loud sound (the hit of a hammer on an iron sheet, like a gong) to observe if the noise frightened the child. Indeed, he was. Albert became frightened and broke into tears after hearing the loud sound produced by the hit of the hammer on the metal sheet.

Having observed the effects of the two stimuli (mouse and sound) when produced separately, the experiment went on to the next phase. Then, a series of presentations began in which the iron sheet was hit with the hammer causing Albert to become scared, while at the same time he was being shown the white mouse.

After this series of presentations, designed to associate the mouse and noise, only the mouse was presented to Albert.

At that time, Watson and Rayner found out that the experiment had been successful, because the child would cry with fear in the mere presence of the rodent.

They had managed to condition little Albert. Prior to the experiment, the mouse did not induce a negative reaction, yet was now a conditioned stimulus, causing fear and crying.

But the conditioning was now so intense that Albert generalized it, showing the same conditioned reaction to the stimuli shown to him at the beginning of the experiment. After the conditioning, he displayed fear reaction in the presence of similar furry objects such as a rabbit, a dog, a monkey and a coat.

End of the experiment

It is not entirely known why, but Albert was removed from the study before he could be deconditioned.

It is believed his mother decided to remove him after becoming concerned about the effects the experiment were having on her son. While her actions were likely well intentioned, she either ignored or was unaware of the power of classical conditioning.

If Watson and Rayner wanted to decondition Albert, they did not get the opportunity.

Even today, Little Albert's identity remains a mystery. Over the years, researchers have tried to discover his full name, how much he was affected by the conditioning as he grew up and how the rest of his life turned out. But although some claimed to have discovered evidence of the child's life, including rumors he had become an adult with a phobia for people, animals or objects with white hair, the reality is there was no solid evidence to support any of these claims. So it is not known whether Albert managed to overcome his conditioning or if it affected his entire life.

Consequences

Today there is no disagreement the experiment lacked ethics. But at the time, many saw it as evidence behavior is learned, and so, with suitable means, anyone could be taught 'proper' behavior.

This principle would influence many later psychological procedures designed to treat mental disorders, such as phobias (irrational fears of certain situations). But beyond mental disorders, it influenced diverse fields, from military training to the development of educational activities and programs.

References

Watson, J.B. & Rayner, R. (1920). *Conditioned emotional reactions.* Journal of Experimental Psychology, Vol 3, No 1, pp. 1–14. doi: 10.1037/h0069608

DOCUMENTARY SOURCES

Bartlett, T. (2014, June 2, 2014). *The Search for Psychology's Lost Boy: In 2009 the decades-old mystery of 'Little Albert' was finally solved. Or was it?* The Chronicle of Higher Education. Consulted on http://chronicle.com/article/ The-Search-for-Psychologys/146747

Beck, H. P., Levinson, S., & Irons, G. (2009). *Finding Little Albert: A journey to John B. Watson's infant laboratory.* American Psychologist, Vol 64, No 7, pp. 605–614. doi: 10.1037/a0017234

Cherry, K. (2014). *The Little Albert Experiment. A Closer Look at the Famous Case of Little Albert.* Chicago, IL: About.com. Consulted on http://psychology.about.com/ od/classicpsychologystudies/a/little-albert-experiment.htm

Fridlund, A. J., Beck, H. P., Goldie, W. D., & Irons, G. (2012). *Little Albert: A neurologically impaired child.* History of Psychology. doi: 10.1037/a0026720

Watson, J. B. & Rayner, R. (2000). *Conditioned emotional reactions.* American Psychologist, Vol 55(3), pp. 313-317. doi: 10.1037/0003-066X.55.3.313

Watson, J. B., & Morgan, J. J. B. (1917). *Emotional Reactions and Psychological Experimentation.* American Journal of Psychology, Vol 28, pp. 163-174. doi: 10.2307/1413718

ASCH EXPERIMENT: THE POWER OF THE GROUP

Unlike some of the experiments we have looked at so far, those of Solomon Asch, performed in 1951, did not have any ethical problems. However the conclusions of this experiment scare me more than any other.

The author

Solomon Asch (1907-1996) was a Polish-born American professor in the Department of Psychology at Swarthmore College in Pennsylvania (US).

The experiment is part of the field of Social Psychology. It aimed to determine the degree of influence group opinion has on individual opinion, i.e., how much a person is able to maintain their own view when everyone around expresses a different opinion.

To answer this question, Professor Asch came up with a simple and clever experiment based on lines painted on cards, along with the help of students and collaborators.

The experiment

The participants were students who had volunteered for what they believed would be a perception test. However, this was a deception, necessary to conceal the real purpose of the experiment.

Each participant was taken to a classroom with several other students. Except for one participant (the experimental subject), the other students were accomplices in the experiment. These accomplices came with previously prepared responses, while the subject of the experiment was completely unaware of their true intent.

Once in the classroom, the experimenter showed the participants a series of cards. A vertical straight line was drawn on the left side of each, while several vertical lines of different sizes were drawn on the right side.

Example of a card from Asch Experiment.

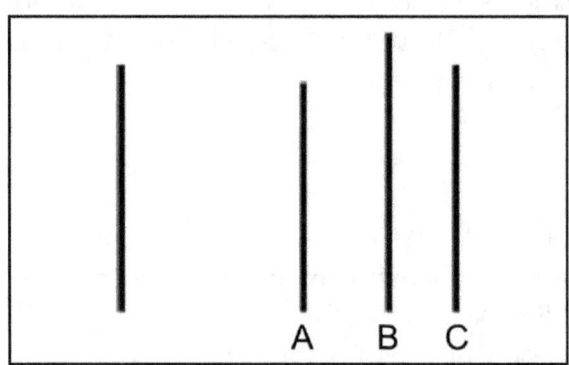

Then the experimenter asked everyone to say which among of the lines on the right was the same size as the one on the left. They had to make a choice between three alternatives.

A total of 18 similar presentations were showed. Initially the accomplices gave correct answers for the purpose of making the experimental subject feel comfortable giving his independent judgement. But from the third presentation the accomplices began giving incorrect answers, sometimes unanimously to put psychological pressure on the experimental subject whose turn was among the last. The accomplices gave wrong answers in 12 out of 18 presentations.

Control group

There was a control group where there were no accomplices and all participants were experimental subjects. The purpose of this control group was to determine the normal percentage of error for the 18 presentations, which was found to be approximately 1%.

But a very different result was obtained from the experimental group, in which the accomplices, with their wrong answers, exerted psychological pressure on the subjects of the experiment.

Results

Asch and his team found the experimental subjects were initially confused by the accomplices' wrong answers, but quickly adapted their response to fit in with the group, by giving the same incorrect answers despite knowing they were not right.

Thus, almost 75% of experimental subjects gave the same answer as the rest of the group in cases where it was wrong.

The experimenters carried out tests varying the number of accomplices who answered incorrectly, and found that as the number of people who gave the wrong answer increased, the probability of the experimental subjects adapting their response to be in line with their teammates also increased. The more people who gave an opinion, the more likely others, who were in the minority, accepted it, even though they disagreed.

Conclusions

The results of this experiment show humans tend to submit their own opinion to the group's opinion. Even when we know the group's opinion is not correct, we give in and accept it, maybe because of fear of being excluded or that our difference of opinion brings us problems or confrontations with others.

So, if a sufficient number of people decided to make a wrong judgment, whatever the issue, a large percentage of people will tend to accept it, and to act according to that view even if they know within themselves it is wrong.

You can imagine the consequences and implications this characteristic of human psychology can have in areas in which we interact daily, as groups of friends, at work or, by adopting a broader point of view, at a social level.

From a different perspective, Asch Experiment also shows the courage and independence of any person who decides not to give in to group psychological pressure, but expresses their own views and behaves according to their own judgment, even if this may entail exclusion or marginalization.

Anyone who is able to maintain their integrity under similar circumstances to the experimental conditions we have seen here, has fought and won a great battle against internal impulses and psychological mechanisms against which many others are unable to resist.

References

Asch, S. (1956). *Studies of independence and conformity: A minority of one against a unanimous majority.* Psychological Monographs, Vol 70, No 9, pp. 1–70. doi: 10.1037/h0093718

DOCUMENTARY SOURCES

Cherry, K. (2014). *The Asch Conformity Experiments*. Chicago, IL: About.com. Consulted on http://psychology.about.com/od/classicpsychologystudies /p/conformity.htm

Swarthmore College (2014). *Swarthmore College*. Swarthmore, PA: Swarthmore College. Consulted on http://www.swarthmore.edu/psychology/solomon-asch-award

THE ROSENHAN EXPERIMENT: ARE WE ALL INSANE?

To this day, the Rosenhan Experiment is one of the biggest criticisms made of institutions dedicated to the care of people suffering from mental illness.

Basically, Rosenhan's research proved a psychiatric institution cannot distinguish the insane from the sane people. This may sound funny at first but when thought about carefully, is extremely worrying.

The author

David L. Rosenhan (1929-2012) was an American professor at Stanford University, with a PhD in Psychology from Columbia University.

Rosenhan was a pioneer in the application of psychological assessment techniques for jury selection. Author of numerous books and research articles, he was popularly known by this experiment, published in 1973 in the journal Science under the title *On Being Sane in Insane Places*.

The experiment

The Professor Rosenhan experiment was conducted in the late nineteen sixties. It consisted of eight people (called *pseudopatients*), who were mentally healthy, but pretended to suffer a psychological disorder in order to get accepted as patients in psychiatric hospitals. Once inside, they had to convince the hospital staff they were sane and get a medical discharge from the doctors.

The study involved the collaboration of eight pseudopatients (three women and five men), who after pretending to suffer auditory hallucinations (claiming to have heard voices), successfully managed to be admitted into several American psychiatric hospitals.

Once admitted, the pseudopatients stop pretending and started to behave normally, saying they did not suffer hallucinations anymore. But even so, they were still forced to admit they were insane and even to accept some kind of treatment.

After nearly a month of average stay (between 7 and 52 days) in their psychiatric hospitals all the pseudopatients were finally discharged. Their supervising doctors all declared their disorder was *"in remission."* None of the participants were discovered, and what is more worrying, none was ever qualified as *"sane."*

A second part of the experiment: the challenge

Once the experiment results were made public, revealing deficiencies in the existing way of diagnosing mental illness, one hospital challenged Rosenhan to send them pseudopatients whenever he liked and without any warning, confident the professor's collaborators would be quickly unmasked by the institution's professionals.

The challenge was accepted. 41 out of the 200 patients received by the new hospital in the weeks after Rosenhan accepted the challenge were rated as pseudopatients, that is, healthy people pretending to suffer a mental disorder.

But Rosenhan had again demonstrated the inefficacy of the diagnoses of psychiatric hospitals of that time, as he had astutely decided to not send any of his collaborators. So all those diagnosed as healthy, probably had real true mental problems.

These results raised even more doubts than the original experiment as to the frequency of incorrect diagnoses made by psychiatric hospitals.

Conclusions

This experiment shows that the practical application of any theory or method always involves a deviation, in many cases due to the human factor.

Although, theoretically, mental illness can be very well defined and categorized, and designed methods considered valid for its diagnosis, the reality is in practice it is not always easy to make accurate diagnoses. Therefore, mistakes are made, perhaps due to faults in the established diagnostic categories, the tools used to diagnose, or just human error, who in many cases are driven by the institution's culture in which they work and are biased with their diagnostic tests results.

This experiment calls into question the role and importance of psychiatric institutions. But more worryingly, of the diagnostic categories themselves, by which people are labeled as *sane* or *insane*, thus socially marking them.

In light of the results from Professor Rosenhan's research, the concepts of sanity and insanity clearly appear like a human creation, which often responds to different reasons than those existing when the original intention of classifying mental illness was carried out.

Perhaps, before rushing to label a person, all of us, both mental health professionals and the general public, should reflect on what mental alterations and disorders actually are. They are no more than deviations from the common and they should not become stigmas to classify people as 'insane', with the personal and social burden this entails.

But this view does not ignore the fact these deviations may require suitable treatment, considering the suffering they cause to both the patient and relatives.

Curiosities

Rosenhan himself was one of the pseudopatients. The other collaborators were a recently graduated psychology student, three psychologists, a pediatrician, a psychiatrist, a painter and a housewife.

The most frequent diagnoses they receive for their 'interpretation' were schizophrenia and manic-depressive disorder.

Interesting enough the actual patients in the psychiatric hospital were the first to suspect the pseudopatients of falsifying their mental illness, even before the physicians did (probably because the pseudopatients were observed taking notes of everything that was happening, just like reporters or professors do).

To be discharged from the hospitals, pseudopatients had to accept a diagnosis of illness and consent to receive medication.

The experiment was important not only for exposing the way mental illness was diagnosed in those days, but also because it called attention to the inhuman conditions in which patients in psychiatric hospitals were treated.

One last thought

From a cursory reading of the experimental results one might conclude the distinction between being 'sane' and what is commonly referred to as 'crazy' is not so clear cut.

And if one concludes the diagnostic classification of mental illness is not reliable, does this mean there is little distinction between being 'sane' or 'insane'? Maybe we are all sane, or, to be tendentious ... could it be we are all a little crazy, in a certain sense?

I have my opinion about that. What is yours?

References

Rosenhan, D. L. (1973). *On Being Sane in Insane Places*. Science, Vol 179, No 4070, pp. 250-258, doi: 10.1126/science.179.4070.250

DOCUMENTARY SOURCES

Romero, J. (June 11, 2012). *David L. Rosenhan, Professor of Law and Psychology, Emeritus.* Stanford, CA: The Board of Trustees of Leland Stanford Junior University. Consulted on http://stanfordlawyer.law.stanford.edu/2012/06/david-l-rosenhan-%E2%80%A8professor-of-law-%E2%80%A8and-psychology-emeritus

THE LEARNED HELPLESSNESS EXPERIMENT: WHEN SOMEONE CANNOT TAKE IT ANYMORE

The learned helplessness behavior was discovered by psychologists Martin Seligman and Steve F. Maier in an experiment designed to investigate how fear influences the learning of escape or avoidance behaviors.

This discovery made them to coin the term and develop the *Theory of Learned Helplessness*.

The authors

Martin E.P. Seligman (New York, 1942) is an American professor of psychology at the University of Pennsylvania. He is mainly known for his contribution to the creation of the branch of psychology called *Positive Psychology* and the discovery of the learned helplessness behavior.

Positive Psychology tries to apply the research and scientific methodology to human traits which so far have not been subjected to a rigorous study, such as happiness, well-being, love, artistic interpretation and even fundamental questions such as the meaning of life.

Steven F. Maier (New York, 1943) is Professor of Psychology at the University of Colorado and Director of the Center for Neuroscience. He has developed his research career in two main areas: how the brain and the immune system interact, and how stress affects brain chemistry. It is within this second line of research he and Professor Seligman devised an experiment in which learned helplessness was discovered.

The experiment

Seligman and Maier published their discovery of Learned Helplessness Behavior in 1967 in the Journal of Experimental Psychology (Seligman and Maier, 1967).

For their experiment, the psychologists used 24 dogs, divided into three groups of eight animals. All of them were fastened with straps, so they could not escape but were able to make certain movements.

The first group was assigned to be the control group, so the animals in it were not subjected to any test. Simply they were tied up or locked up, to be released after some time.

The dogs of the second group were administered a series of electrical discharges (experimenters said discharges were *"painful but not harmful"*). The animals could not escape because they were tied up, but if they pressed a panel with their heads, discharges ceased, so that the dogs 'learned' they had control over the pain received.

Finally, the dogs in the third group were also subject to the discharges, but in this case they were in company of one of the dogs from the second group, those who 'knew' how to stop the pain. But discharges only ceased when the dog from the second group pressed the panel. If the dog belonging to the third group did so, electric currents did not stop. No matter what the animal did, even though it was the same action as to what gave good results to its partner, it had no control over the punishment received.

After several hours following this procedure, the dogs were taken to the second part of the experiment.

Second part

In the second part of the study, the dogs, one by one, were introduced into a cage. The cage had some lights on in its sides. The lights were then switch off for ten seconds. During this time an electric discharge was administered. While the lights were out, the cage door was left open and the dogs had an opportunity to escape.

The dogs from the second group (who had learned to stop the discharges by pressing a panel in the first part of the experiment) quickly realized a relationship existed between the lights being off and the beginning of the discharge. After a few trials, they all learned that by escaping from the cage they could avoid an electric shock.

But dogs from the third group, who in the first part of the experiment had continued receiving electric shocks no matter what they did, showed much less learning ability. Nearly 80% failed to escape from the cage to prevent discharges after the lights went out, and the few who learned a way to escape took almost twice as long to learn than the dogs from the second group.

Conclusions

The results show that living beings (other experiments have allowed these findings to be generalized to include humans) when perceiving their attempts to solve a problem do not work, eventually fall into a psychological state of learned helplessness, where they abandon themselves to the situation and make no further effort to resolve it.

This state is a psychological characteristic that defines animals and people. Maybe some endure more than others a stressful situation and make further attempts to resolve it, but, at some moment, everyone has a breaking point, where we assume whatever we do is not going to change the situation, so we resign ourselves to accepting it. At that point, although a solution may be clearly presented to us, we will be unable to take it rather stay immersed in the helplessness state.

Learned helplessness and depression

The state of learned helplessness is often associated with depression. For this reason, most people, despite their good intentions toward someone who is depressed, may use expressions such as *"come on," "you need to do something to get motivated," "try harder," "you'll see as time goes by you'll feel better."* But they do not understand someone with depression is in a different psychological state to others, and is actually in learned helplessness.

Anyone can reach this state of learned helplessness and fall into depression after trying many different ways to escape a bad situation without success.

To overcome this state of mind conventional solutions do not work. Even though all it might take to beat the depression is to cross a threshold, the sufferer will not do it because, just as the dogs of the third group learned, whatever he or she did would not provide escape from the pain.

It is important to understand learned helplessness so as to not blame people when they fall into it. It must be seen as a psychological mechanism present in all of us, which will be activated if sufficient pressure is applied.

I believe keep this in mind would be helpful for our competitive societies to not label people *winner, loser, successful* or *failed.*

Learned helplessness is not a choice or the result of a weak character or lack of will, it is a defining characteristic of the psychology of animals and people, so it is present in all of us. Anyone can fall into a state of learned helplessness if their resources fail to overcome external pressures. Sometimes you simply cannot take it anymore.

References

Seligman, M.E.P. & Maier, S.F. (1967). *Failure to escape traumatic shock.* Journal of Experimental Psychology, Vol 74, pp. 1–9. doi: 10.1037/h0024514

DOCUMENTARY SOURCES

Seligman, M. E. P. (1975). *Helplessness: On Depression, Development, and Death.* San Francisco: W. H. Freeman.

SEPP (2011). *Sociedad española de psicología positiva.* Consulted on http://www.sepsicologiapositiva.es

Smallheer, B. A. (2011). *Learned helplessness and depressive symptoms in patients following acute myocardial infarction.* Nashville, Tennessee: Inédito. Recovered from http://etd.library.vanderbilt.edu/available/etd-03152011-210853/unrestricted/Final_Dissertation_Combination.pdf

University of Colorado (2014). *Neuroscience. University of Colorado at Boulder.* Denver, CO: Regents of University of Colorado. Consulted on http://www.colorado.edu/neuroscienceprogram/maier.html

BARTLETT EXPERIMENT: DO NOT TRUST YOUR MEMORY

The Bartlett Experiment, also known as the Bartlett Story, shows us very clearly how unreliable human memory is, and how we should think twice before trusting our own memory or to something anyone, even with the best of intentions, tell us.

Sir Frederic Charles Bartlett

Frederic Bartlett (1886-1969) was a British psychologist, professor of Experimental Psychology at the University of Cambridge.. He gained posterity for his studies on cognitive psychology and memory. His most influential work is *Remembering: A Study in Experimental and Social Psychology* (Bartlett, 1932).

He was a member of the prestigious Royal Society, and in 1948, in recognition of his collaboration with the Royal Air Force during World War II, he was awarded a knighthood, which allowed him to hold the very British title of "Sir."

The Barlett Story

Bartlett's intention with this experiment was to investigate the process of remembrance and how well people remember things. It was a very simple and easily reproducible experiment which most readers will find the results acceptable.

To learn how the process of remembering works, Bartlett devised the following experiment:

He asked the participants to read a short story, an old Native American legend entitled *War of the Ghosts*.

Once read, Bartlett asked them, on different occasions, to re-tell it, waiting increasing time intervals between each telling, in order to see how the passing of time influenced the formation of memories.

As time passed, each story became more different from the original one. Every one of the participants, on each occasion were asked to re-tell the story, tended to substitute important details by others, usually influenced by their personality, past experiences and cultural background.

War of the Ghosts

This was the original story read by the participants of the experiment:

One night two young men from Egulac went down to the river to hunt seals and while they were there it became foggy and calm. Then they heard war-cries, and they thought: "Maybe this is a war-party." They escaped to the shore, and hid behind a log.

Now canoes came up, and they heard the noise of paddles, and saw one canoe coming up to them. There were five men in the canoe, and they said:

"What do you think? We wish to take you along. We are going up the river to make war on the people."

One of the young men said, "I have no arrows."

"Arrows are in the canoe," they said.

"I will not go along. I might be killed. My relatives do not know where I have gone. But you," he said, turning to the other, "may go with them."

So one of the young men went, but the other returned home.

And the warriors went on up the river to a town on the other side of Kalama. The people came down to the water and they began to fight, and many were killed.

But presently the young man heard one of the warriors say, "Quick, let us go home: that Indian has been hit." Now he thought: "Oh, they are ghosts." He did not feel sick, but they said he had been shot.

So the canoes went back to Egulac and the young man went ashore to his house and made a fire. And he told everybody and said: "Behold I accompanied the ghosts, and we went to fight. Many of our fellows were killed, and many of those who attacked us were killed. They said I was hit, and I did not feel sick."

He told it all, and then he became quiet. When the sun rose he fell down. Something black came out of his mouth. His face became contorted. The people jumped up and cried.

He was dead.

Some distortions of the story

As Bartlett proved with his experiment, as time passed since the short story was read, participants tended to alter it, introducing distortions according to their personal characteristics. That is, memories were customized by their mental schemes.

Some of the most common effects of time on remembering the story were the omissions of data or to modify or replace important details in accordance with their own life experience.

So, some of the participants, when they could not remember the name of the village the young men belonged to

(Egulac), replaced it saying they were from "*a tribe*." Others omitted details such as before the arrival of the canoes the two men had heard the sound of oars, or that before one of them agreed to accompany the warriors there was a conversation about arrows. Other times, some of the story elements were substituted by others more familiar to the participants, for example instead of referring to canoes they spoke of "*boats*."

Conclusions

Summarizing, people alter their memories to adapt them to their view of the world and to their experience. The more time has passed since the situation we want to remember happened, the higher the probability we have distorted it in our minds. When remembering, we do not just recall a memory, but each time we remember we build a new one, altering and differentiating it from the original.

In this simple way Bartlett proved that our way of being, our way of thinking (the way we interpret the world) and the passing of time largely determine how we create our memories.

References

Bartlett, F.C. (1920). *Some experiments on the reproduction of folk stories.* Folk-Lore 31: 30-47.

DOCUMENTARY SOURCES

Bartlett, F. C. (1932). *Remembering: A Study in Experimental and Social Psychology.* Cambridge, UK: Cambridge University Press.

Bartlett, F. C. (1995). *Remembering. A Study in Experimental and Social Psychology.* Cambridge: Cambridge University Press.

Duveen, G., Gillespie, A. & Wagoner, B. (2014). *Sir Frederic Bartlett Archive.* Cambridge, Department of Psychology, University of Cambridge: Duveen, G., Gillespie, A. & Wagoner, B. Consulted on http://www.bartlett.psychol.cam.ac.uk/index.html

THE ROBBERS CAVE EXPERIMENT: THE REASONS OF HATE BETWEEN GROUPS

The Robbers Cave State Park was chosen by the Turkish psychologist Muzafer Sherif (1906-1988) and his wife, Carolyn W. Sherif (1922-1982), also a psychologist, in 1954 to perform a famous experiment in social psychology, which came to be known as the Robbers Cave Experiment.

Robbers Cave State Park

Robbers Cave State Park is an area of natural beauty, in hilly woodlands of Sans Bois Mountains, South East Oklahoma (US), covering 30 square kilometers. Today is a favorite location for camping, hiking, climbing, fishing and horseback riding.

But back in the nineteenth century, the natural conditions of the cave, which today gives its name to the whole park (hidden in a large wooded and mountainous area, with natural water flows and an opportune rear exit) made this area an ideal hiding place for outlaws of the American Wild West, including the famous Jesse James and the Dalton Gang.

It was to this isolated area, some 60 kilometers from the nearest town, the Sherifs brought 22 children to conduct their famous experiment. The experiment was to investigate how group relations work and the causes of conflict between them.

The experiment

The experiment was developed in 1954, as part of a study by the University of Oklahoma to investigate the nature of relations between groups of people. It was conducted in an old Boy Scout summer camp within the Robbers Cave State Park.

The experimental subjects were 22, 12-year-old, middle class children, with similar level of education, who did not know each other. The experiment lasted three weeks and consisted of three phases:

1.– Group formation.
2.– Friction.
3.– Integration.

In the first phase, two different groups were formed, and sent to different areas of the camp so as to not interact with one another.

In the second phase, the friction phase, a series of games and reward activities were implemented in which the two groups competed against each other.

In the third phase, integration, group activities were not directed to competition but cooperation, so to perform them both groups had to work together.

Now we will see what happened in each phase of the Robbers Cave Experiment.

First phase: Group formation

During the initial phase the two groups of the experiment were formed.

Each child was assigned to one of the groups based on the results of psychological tests and other factors such as height, weight, sports and games abilities, etc. So, each group was composed of children who were as similar as possible.

None of the children were aware of the existence of the other group of children in the area. They would meet for the first time in the next phase. To retain their ignorance of the other's group presence, each one arrived at the camp on a different day and was assigned a different area to settle.

The members of each group quickly began to unite, performing various tasks to achieve common objectives (such as making a barbecue, organizing a swimming area, painting signs, etc.). To do this, they had to plan, make decisions and take actions. This promoted order, cooperation and collaboration in both groups.

The experimenters, playing the role of summer camp guards, found leaders soon emerged, and groups tended to organize themselves hierarchically, in order to perform tasks in a more organized way.

Second phase: Friction between groups

During the second phase, experimenters created tension between the two groups of children by making the groups compete against each other in games and sports competitions. So, friction was created between the groups out of the frustration of the losing group for failing to win.

The researchers observed negative attitudes emerging between the groups, such as boasts about how one may be better athletes than the other, jokes about failures of their rivals and so on. Group identity began to form as each group talked about 'their' areas of the camp. Each group marked its territory.

A banner created by one group for a baseball game clearly demonstrated the creation of group identity and of hostilities towards the other. It said: "YOU CAN WIN THE MATCH BUT WE ARE GOING TO GIVE YOU A HELL OF A FIGHT."

Third phase: Group integration

The last phase of the experiment tried to reduce the differences between the groups which had resulted from the previous phase. To achieve this, two mechanisms were used.

The first made exchanges between members of the groups for a limited time. In these cases, it was found that communication and knowing each other did not diminish negative attitudes between them. It did not matter that a child spent some time with the other group, he was still perceived as "different" and "a rival."

The second method used to eliminate the negative feelings between the two groups was to make them cooperate to achieve a common goal. This common objective, such as repairing the water tank supplying them, was something of importance to both groups.

The experimenters observed that when working together to achieve a goal, the groups tended to stop seeing each other as rivals and began developing positive inter-group relationships.

Conclusions

From observations made during the third phase, the Sherif's drew several conclusions including:

1.– When two groups are forced to compete with each other to achieve goals or objectives, the sense of belonging to one group is emphasized and hostility toward the other increases. In a situation of this type prejudices, discrimination and the feeling of being different come easily.

2.– Contact between groups, by itself, does not reduce hostility. Only when two groups are able to work together to achieve a goal of common interest, both hostile feelings and behaviors disappear. Collaboration and cooperation actions minimize prejudices and distinction attitudes existing between groups of people.

In summary, it is not differences between people which creates hostility or a feeling of friendship between groups, but more practical issues such as competition or cooperation, which determines the nature of intergroup relations and the attitudes, prejudices and feelings of one group of people to members of another group.

Attitudes such as xenophobia, racism or discrimination exist not because people really think individual differences are important, but because different groups with particular practical goals are created and people do not perceive there to be common goals between them. This is the main reason prejudices, segregation and exclusion are abundant in conflicts between groups of human beings.

An example of the utility of this discovery

These results have been made good use of on many occasions. Nelson Mandela provided a good example of how to use a common goal to resolve conflicts between groups, after the years of racial segregation in South Africa, known as *Apartheid*.

After spending 25 years in prison, he eventually became president of South Africa in 1994. Then, in 1995 the Rugby

World Cup was held in his country, offering him the perfect opportunity to provide a common cause.

Until then, rugby was considered an exclusive sport of the dominant white class. But he tirelessly showed support for the national team, the Springboks, and promoted rugby among oppressed groups.

By the end of the campaign most of the country supported the national team, and on June 24, 1995, at Ellis Park, Johannesburg, the South African team beat the all-powerful New Zealand team.

To many this victory played an important role in the complex reconciliation of antagonistic groups, allowing all people of South Africa to share a sense of national identity regardless of race or social position.

Curiosities

In contrast with other experiments, although the research team was not to interfere with relations created between the two groups, they were warned to not neglect the health and safety of the children.

Both groups had very appropriate names considering they were in a camp located in the Boy Scouts lands. One was called Rattlers and the other Eagles.

It is popularly believed ill-gotten gains of the outlaws of the old American Wild West still lie hidden in Robbers Cave State Park. Perhaps if during the experiment someone had found some of this treasure, Carolyn and Muzafer Sherif could have added another variable to their study of the causes of hostility between human groups.

References

Sherif, M., Harvey, O. J. White, B. J., Hood, W. R. & Sherif, C.W. (1961). *Intergroup Conflict and Cooperation: The Robbers Cave Experiment*. Norman, OK: University of Oklahoma.

DOCUMENTARY SOURCES

Barber, G., Birnbaum, R., Eastwood, C., Freeman, M., Hofmeyr, G., Lorenz, R., McCreary, L., Moore, T. & Neufeld, M. (producers) & Eastwood, C. (director) (2009). *Invictus*. [Movie film]. USA: Warner Bros. (presents), Spyglass Entertainment (in association with), Revelations Entertainment (as Revelations Entertainment/Man Company), Malpaso Productions, Liberty Pictures y Mace Neufeld Productions (uncredited).

Oklahoma Tourism & Recreation Department (2014). Oklahoma. Robbers Cave State Park. Oklahoma: Oklahoma Tourism & Recreation Department. Consulted on http://www.travelok.com/listings/view.profile/id.6415

Wilson, S. (1989). *Oklahoma Treasures and Treasure Tales*. Norman, OK: University of Oklahoma Press.

THE SMALL WORLD EXPERIMENT: IS THIS REALLY A SMALL WORLD?

This experiment was performed in 1969 by Stanley Milgram (New York University) and Jeffrey Travers (PhD in Social Relations from Harvard University). The study tried to assess the validity of the commonly used expression "it's a small world!"

This expression suggests it is easy to find unknown people who has or has had some kind of relationship with someone we know, or we can sometimes meet someone we know at an unexpected place.

Milgram and Travers intended to give a scientific answer to this popular belief, trying to find out which is the probability two people living in different cities share a connection through other people, some of them completely strangers to one or both of them.

Background

Stanley Milgram was already famous for the experiment conducted in the early 1960s to investigate the basis of obedience to authority, which we discussed in a previous chapter.

The question of what is the separation degree between people in society (in real social networks, not virtual, which did not exist then) had already been posed in the past, but Milgram carried out a series of tests to scientifically investigate it.

The results of those researches were published in 1967 in an article in the Psychology Today magazine, titled *The Small-World Problem*, article that caused a great interest among the public.

However, in this chapter we will see in a general way (as always, I refer the reader to the original papers for further details) the experiment described in the article published along with Jeffrey Travers, titled *An Experimental Study of the Small World Problem*, released in 1969 in the Sociometry Journal. This article is considered more rigorous and detailed than the previous one, because it was published in a specialized journal.

The experiment

The participants in the study were asked to send letters to friends in order to make contact with a particular person, completely unknown to them, who lived in a different city.

At first it might seem very difficult, if not impossible, for someone to make contact with a particular stranger living many miles or kilometers away using only a network of friends and acquaintances. But the results of this experiment showed it is not that difficult.

In fact, based the results, it seems the world is even smaller than anyone thought. Using this method, almost 30% of participants' letters reached the assigned person. While this result may not seem very high, it is when compared to what might have originally thought.

Just imagine you are asked to locate someone you do not know, who lives in a different city, and you have to do it by only sending letters to people you know. What chances do you think your letter would have of ever reaching its intended addressee?

The procedure

The experimental method had been previously developed by Stanley Milgram, and was known as *Small World Method*. It was the procedure he used for the experiments he described in the 1967 article published in the Psychology Today magazine.

The Small World Method and its namesake experiment are as follows:

296 people residing in the US cities of Nebraska and Boston were selected as participants. Then, they were asked to attempt to contact a stranger who lived in another city. The city in which the unknown person lived was Massachusetts. The participants were only allowed to use relatives, friends and acquaintances to get the letter to its destination.

Each participant was given a letter in which the reasons and the conditions of the study were explained. The participant had to send it to a person who he or she knew and thought might be useful in getting it closer to the final addressee. The person who received the letter had to send it to another, while fulfilling the same conditions, and so on, until it hopefully reached its intended target. If the addressee at the end of the chain received the letter, he or she was to send it back to the experimenters.

Basically, the study objectives were: 1) find out whether the letter reached its intended destination, and 2) if so, how many people were needed to get it to the target person. To determine the latter, everyone receiving a letter was to fill in their details before sending it to the next person.

The letter was only to be sent to a known person who they thought could help getting it closer to the final addressee. Nobody could send the letter directly to the final recipient unless they knew him or her personally.

Results

217 out the 296 study participants made the first sending of the letter. 64 of those sent reached their final destination, so the success rate was almost 30%.

In addition to this success rate, it should be noted in many cases letters successfully reaching their intended destination had passed through the same hands more than once. So although each letter was sent by a different participant, it sometimes passed again through the same person, thus confirming the world is indeed a small place.

In where cases letters eventually made it to their intended address, the average number of people composing the chain was 5.2, i.e., the number of people separating two completely strangers from different cities (the original sender and the final addressee) was less than 6.

Do your own experiment

No doubt, had social networking methods, such as Facebook, existed at the time of the Milgram and Travers experiment, they would have been part of the experimental method.

So, using more modern methods you might try your own experiment to see how big or small the world is. If you have a Facebook profile, do some research among your friends to determine unknown common relationships. For example, how many who do not know each other share common friends with you.

This is a very quick and simple way to check for yourself if the world is as small as Milgram and Travers suggested a few years ago with their more limited resources.

References

Milgram, S. (1967). *The Small-World Problem.* Psychology Today, Vol 1, No 1, pp. 61- 67. doi: 10.2307/2786545

Travers, J. & Milgram, S. (1969). *An Experimental Study of the Small World Problem.* Sociometry, Vol 32, No. 4, pp. 425-443. doi: 10.2307/2786545

DOCUMENTARY SOURCES

Harvard University (2007). *The Department of Psychology.* Cambridge, MA: President and Fellows of Harvard College. Consulted on http://www.isites.harvard.edu/ icb/icb.do?keyword=k3007&pageid=icb.page28893

LANDIS EXPERIMENT OF FACIAL EXPRESSIONS: THE FACE IS THE MIRROR OF THE SOUL?

In 1924, Carney Landis, a graduate of psychology from the University of Minnesota, designed and conducted an experiment to see if emotions were accompanied by specific facial expressions.

The experiment

The experiment involved volunteers (students and Landis' university fellows, along with himself). They were all painted with a series of stripes across their faces.

The lines were marked in the areas of the face which articulate facial expressions, such as eyebrows, cheeks, lips, chin and nose. The lines enabled Landis to measure the gestural variations occurring between different emotions, among different people.

To trigger emotional reactions in the participants, Landis subjected them to various stimuli. Some of the most striking included smelling ammonia, putting their hands into baskets of frogs and showing them erotic images.

With these tests, Landis sought to generate emotions in the subjects, such as disgust, fear, joy or surprise.

But in his attempt to get arouse emotional reactions, Landis conceived the most controversial part of the experiment. At a certain point in the test, the psychologist asked the participants to behead a rat.

What happened then?

One third of the participants refused to perform the request when this point was reached, while the others agreed to follow the experimenter's instructions.

Determined to continue the investigation even though some of the subjects refused to follow his orders, Landis forced them to watch while someone else did it, in order to study the emotional reaction shown in their faces.

Results

With his experiment Landis intended to open a door to the emotional world of humans.

Emotions and feelings are very complex, and it is almost impossible to know the emotional state of a person for certain. Landis probably thought we could know the emotional state of someone by analyzing their facial expression.

The implications of such a discovery go far beyond the simple benefit of better communication between people. If each emotion carries a certain facial expression, then by conveniently analyzing gestures we could know what emotion a particular situation induces in people: the way a professor teaches a lesson, a lecturer dissertation, the design of a consumable product, showing evidence to someone accused of a crime, or a police interrogation of a suspect are just some of the practical applications where it would be useful to know what facial gesture comes with each emotion. These may be some of the possibilities Carney Landis had in mind when designing his experiment.

Conclusions

Landis Experiment was not successful because he did not obtain sufficient results to confirm his hypothesis of the relationship between facial expressions and emotions.

There have been several criticisms made of his research. Obviously, a big concern was the lack of ethics in asking people to do something against their moral code and not respecting their refusal, as well as the flagrant violation of animal rights.

Apart from these objections, there were problems with methodology, such as not establishing a control group (participants not subjected to the test), or not measuring the psychological characteristics of the participants (as each person will react differently to the same situation).

Paul Ekman

Years later, in 1960, psychologist Paul Ekman found an easier way to know if each emotion carries a certain facial expression.

Ekman traveled to Papua New Guinea and established contact with a tribe living completely isolated from modern civilization. Once he had gained their confidence, he showed them a series of photos of people expressing different emotions (joy, anger, disgust, fear, etc.). Ekman could see how the natives recognized some of these expressions because they also used them to express emotions.

In this apparently so simple way, Ekman established the relationship between facial expressions and emotions, and concluded six basic emotions are present in all human beings: joy, sadness, fear, anger, surprise and disgust.

Ekman's experiment changed the understanding of emotions that had existed until then, and has influenced much of the later research on emotions

Curiosities

Reviewing the Landis Experiment, it is often said while it may not have been successful in its objective to know if emotions and facial expressions were associated, it unintentionally served to advance the results of the 1962 Stanley Milgram experiment (which we discussed in an earlier chapter, *Blind Obedience to Authority*).

This experiment, conducted forty year after Landis' study, was to determine the extent to which people have a tendency to obey orders.

The results of Milgram's research showed 65% of participants followed orders to administer an electric shock to a person, under certain conditions. In the Landis experiment, two-thirds of the participants followed his instructions to behead a rat even though the order caused them a deep discomfort. Two thirds are 66% of sample. So Landis and Milgram obtained practically the same result when it came to obedience to authority.

References

Landis, C. (1924). *Studies of emotional reactions. I. A preliminary study of facial expression.* Journal of Experimental Psychology, Vol 7(5), pp. 325-341. doi: 10.1037/h0076072

Landis, C. (1924). *Studies of Emotional Reactions. II. General Behavior and Facial Expression.* Journal of Comparative Psychology, Vol 4(5), pp. 447-510. doi: 10.1037/h0073039

DOCUMENTARY SOURCES

Paul Ekman Group, LLC (2013). *Paulekman.com*. San Francisco, CA: Paul Ekman Group. Consulted on http://www.paulekman.com

HARLOW EXPERIMENTS WITH APES: THE ORIGIN OF LOVE AND THE EFFECTS OF LONELINESS

The experiments of American psychologist Harry Harlow are remembered more by their methods than their results. Performed when ethical standards were far different from now, there is no doubt by today's standards these experiments would be considered unethical.

In this chapter we will look at two of this researcher's most famous experiments, one about the nature of love and the other about the effects of loneliness.

Both studies used Rhesus Macaque monkeys, a species often used for scientific research. The Rh factor (Rh positive or negative) in human blood was discovered as a result of research with Rhesus monkeys. They were also flown into space during America's Project Mercury in the 1950's and 60's, before human missions began.

Harry F. Harlow

Harry Frederick Harlow (1905-1981) studied at Stanford University, and after obtaining a doctorate in psychology, he was hired as professor at the University of Wisconsin.

It was there he founded the Primates Laboratory, where he would carry out his well-known experiments with monkeys in the late 1950's and 60's.

The experiment about the nature of love

With this research Harlow sought to investigate the mechanisms of love. For him, the first and most basic form of love was the attachment between mothers and their children, so he conceived an experiment to study the nature of love of babies for their mothers using his group of monkeys.

For this purpose, Harlow built some "surrogate mothers." They were of two types: the first type was made of wire and simulated the shape of a monkey; these were the *metal mothers*. The second type, also of simian appearance, was covered with a woven structure to simulate monkey fur; these were the *cloth mothers*.

A few newborn babies were separated from their mothers and brought together with the artificial ones. After several months under the 'care' of each type of surrogate mothers, all the young monkeys were put in front of both types, giving them the opportunity to choose between one and the other.

For this situation, the metal mother had been equipped with a feeding bottle so the babies could drink, but the cloth mother did not have one. Harlow found most of the babies tended to spend more time with the second type of surrogate mother, the cloth mother, that provided them warmth and similarity to fur. Occasionally they left to feed from the metal one, but when finished they returned to the cloth mother.

This experiment showed the nature of love between parents and children is more psychological than instinctive, and it is based on natural emotional factors. Simply attending to basic needs, such as providing food, does not necessarily creates love, but it is the satisfaction of emotional needs that constitutes the basis of loving ties and affection. In the case of the monkey babies of the experiment, this was provided by the warm feeling of comfort of the cloth mothers.

This research would serve to give prominence to the role of adoptive parents versus biological parents in adoption cases.

The experiment about the effects of loneliness

With this series of experiments, Harlow and his collaborators investigated the effect prolonged loneliness would have on an individual.

To this end they decided to investigate how isolation affected monkeys, because previous investigations had shown similarities between the individual development of humans and monkeys.

Several groups of monkeys were formed, each one subjected to different conditions of isolation.

One group would be subjected to *partial isolation* by locking them in cages preventing physical contact with their peers, but visual contact was possible, since other monkeys were close to the cage. They could see other monkeys, but not interact with them.

The other group was subjected to *total isolation*, i.e., these monkeys were completely isolated, with no at all contact with their peers.

Both isolation conditions were in periods of three, six and twelve months.

Results

The results revealed loneliness can have traumatic effects on individuals.

Once released, the monkeys showed various behavioral disorders, such as the inability to play, reduced intellectual capacity, difficulty in solving problems or increased fear of other monkeys. The fear of other monkeys was the most prevalent outcome. Even years after their release, some monkeys still suffered severe emotional disorders, such as anorexia.

In the case of those who were in total isolation the effects were accentuated. As Harlow put it, the consequences of isolation were *"devastating"* (Harlow, 1965). Once released, the extreme conditions of isolation had completely removed the ability of the animals to interact with their peers.

Implications

These findings have implications for the understanding of the effects of loneliness on humans. People living a life of loneliness often develop attitudes and behaviors similar to those of Harlow's monkeys.

Understanding the fear of others or aggressive behaviors exhibited by people who have suffered conditions of isolation can help develop programs and treatments to aid their reintegration into society.

The results of Harlow experiment are also useful to comprehend the effects long isolation periods have on people forced to remain alone, either for work (astronauts, scientists and workers at remote locations) or for other reasons (prison inmates or prisoners of war).

The methods

There was much criticism of Harlow's methods due to the mistreatment of animals.

Harlow's methods were controversial. They prompted public debate over the use of animals in experiments and have been cited as a factor in the rise of animal rights groups.

References

Harlow H. F., Dodsworth R.O. & Harlow M.K. (1965). *Total social isolation in monkeys*. Proc Natl Acad Sci USA, Vol. 54 (1), pp. 90–97. Consulted on http://www.ncbi.nlm.nih.gov/pmc/articles/PMC285801/#reference-sec

Harlow, H. F. (1958). *The nature of love*. American Psychologist, Vol 13 (12), pp. 673-685. doi: 10.1037/h0047884

Harlow, H. F. (1959). *Love in Infant Monkeys*. Scientific American, Vol 200, pp. 68, 70, 72-73, 74. doi: 10.1038/scientificamerican0659-68

DOCUMENTARY SOURCES

Cherry, K. (2014). *Harry Harlow Biography (1905-1981).* Chicago, IL: About.com. Consulted on http://psychology.about.com/od/profilesal/p/harry-harlow.htm

Harlow, H.F. & Suomi, S.J. (1970) *Nature of Love: Simplified.* American Psychologist, 25(2), 161-168, doi: 10.1037/h0029383

National Geographic (2013). *Macaco Rhesus.* Washington, D.C.: National Geographic Society. Consulted on http://nationalgeographic.es/animales/mamiferos/macaco-rhesus

Slater, L. (2004, 21 de marzo). *Monkey love. Harry Harlow's classic primate experiments suggest that to understand the human heart you must be willing to break it.* Boston.com, The New York Times Company. Recovered from http://www.boston.com/news/globe/ideas/articles/2004/03/21/monkey_love

KURT LEWIN EXPERIMENT: THE BEST FORM OF GOVERNMENT

The experiment commonly known as Leadership Styles Experiment was conducted by the American psychologist of German origin Kurt Lewin (1890-1947), in 1939.

Lewin and his researchers investigated how group dynamics affects its members and the functioning of the group. Their results had a major impact on Social Psychology, where Lewin is considered a leading figure.

In the experiment we are about to review, we will see how Levin investigated how leadership style influences the behavior of a group's members.

Background

In 1933, Lewin was forced to leave Germany, abandoning his position at the University of Berlin, to escape the increasing spread of Nazism in his country.

His chosen destination, as for so many others, was the United States. Once in America, he worked for several universities, including the University of Iowa.

In those years there was a growing interest in understanding the social mechanisms occurring in Germany, due to concern over the unstoppable rise of National Socialism and how almost the entire German people succumbed to its influence.

These events and life experiences led Kurt Lewin to try to unravel the effects social climates derived from different leadership styles had on people's behavior.

The experiment

This investigation was a continuation of some previous similar experiments. As previous, a group of children aged 8-10 years were used as experimental subjects. How they related to each other, as well as their physical condition and psychological condition was assessed prior to the experiment.

Put simply, Lewin divided the children into several groups with an adult (a collaborator in the experiment) in charge of each group.

All the groups were asked to do a series of manual activities (making theater masks, painting murals, making some toys, etc.). Each collaborator was instructed to apply a different leadership style. The groups' reactions would be observed over a period of three months.

The first group was 'governed' by *autocratic leadership* style, in which the collaborator gave orders and direct instructions and assigned individuals to each task, while showing no receptivity to any kind of suggestions from group members.

A second group was directed using a *liberal leadership* style, in which the children were barely given any instructions on how to organize and perform their assigned tasks. When the adult in charge was asked a question, the collaborator's general attitude was apathy and made no efforts to lead the group.

The third group was ruled with a *democratic leadership* style, in which the collaborator discussed the best way to perform tasks with the children, encouraging participation and asking questions. He gave no direct indications on how to perform tasks, but offered several options to let the children discuss and make decisions by themselves. He gave them freedom to choose their companions in each task and tried to appear as just one more member of the group rather than their leader.

Results

After three months, the collected information was analyzed. The results were based on each group's developed social relationship and its effect on the children's behavior.

Lewin found the children under the autocratic style of leadership became aggressive towards their companions while submissive to the collaborator who played their leader. The group's atmosphere was very competitive, and the children would often fight with each other for attention or to highlight their individual achievements. Criticism and insults of their companions along with selfish attitudes (demanding attention) were often present.

The children belonging to the group with the liberal leadership style sometimes failed to fulfill their given tasks. Rebellious or aggressive attitudes appeared between them, such as blaming others for not getting a task done. With no instructions or support from the collaborator playing their leader, they failed to organize themselves effectively.

The third group, in which a democratic leadership style was used, like the first group (with autocratic leadership) also achieved the objectives, but the difference between the two groups was the atmosphere created among its members. Instead of developing competitive or aggressive behaviors as in the first group, the democratic group showed friendly and participatory behavior in which they helped each other to perform tasks. They had constructive discussions before making decisions and due to their enthusiasm for their tasks, it was not always necessary for the collaborator to be present.

They tended to treat the adult who guided them as an equal partner, and relate to him as if he were one of them

Conclusions

The experiment clearly showed the climate created within a group, by the style of its leader, facilitates certain types of behavior among its members.

The study showed how the behavior of group members is largely influenced by the way it is run. Depending on the leadership style used, one or another type of behaviors and ways of relating between members will emerge.

Lewin's research confirmed the democratic style of leadership had the most positive effect on people's behavior. It not only facilitated the achievement of common goals, but the emergence of positive attitudes, such as equality, cooperation and mutual assistance.

In particular Lewin's findings have had a major influence on the understanding of how affects people the group's atmosphere created by the leadership style with which it is directed. In the field of education, these results are very useful helping educators to design more effective teaching styles and methods.

On a wider scale, when some types of social behavior become widespread, such as submission, aggression, cooperation and many others, it is possible to find an explanation of their origins in terms of how the way society is governed.

Considering how events were folding during the years just prior to the Second World War, in which this experiment took place, Lewin's results were seen as an endorsement of democratic systems of government, as opposed to the authoritarian leadership of Germany, already firmly in place.

They also help to better understand the German people's reactions to Nazi leadership, and how the country would behave in the months and years to come, in a period that tragically and indelibly marked the history of the twentieth century and of all humanity.

Curiosities

The way in which I have explained the experiment is commonly used, and helps describe the results and the intention of the investigation. However, the experiment methodology was more complex than I implied.

There were actually more than three groups, since Lewin also established a control group (one in which studied variables were not applied). Also, he sometimes changed the group leaders, to confirm it was the leadership style and not the leader's personality what created the climate conducive to certain behaviors. And there were phases in which the three types of leadership styles were tested in each of the groups, to compare the influence of the three styles on the same group of children.

In the article describing the investigation, Lewin incorporates the same type of experiments conducted by Ron Lippitt and Robert White.

The liberal style was defined by Lewin with the French expression *laissez-faire*, which translates to something like "let do." However, when the experiment is described the expression *liberal* is often used, because it helps to convey the idea of the research testing leadership styles of political systems.

References

Lewin, K., Lippitt, R. & White, R. K. (1939). *Patterns of aggressive behavior in experimentally created "social climates"*. The Journal of Social Psychology, Vol 10, pp. 271-299. doi: 10.1080/00224545.1939.9713366

DOCUMENTARY SOURCES

Smith, M. K. (2001). *Kurt Lewin: groups, experiential learning and action research*. London: Infed.org, YMCA George Williams College. Consulted on http://infed.org/mobi/kurt-lewin-groups-experiential-learning-and-action-research

THE THIRD WAVE EXPERIMENT: CREATING A TOTALITARIAN STATE IN A WEEK

In 1967, in California, Professor Ron Jones designed a little experiment in social psychology to teach his students how Nazism managed to succeed in Germany during the 1930s.

This experiment, which is actually more of a demonstration because it did not use scientific method principles, became so popular it eventually inspired a TV series, a bestseller, a film, a documentary, a museum and even a musical.

Background

In the spring of 1967, Ron Jones was a twenty-five years old professor of history, teaching at Cubberley High School, Palo Alto (California, US).

Due to the disbelief of his students when he described the social situation in Germany during the Nazi era, the young teacher decided to show them, through a practical experiment, how easily a country could become a totalitarian state.

But as had happened on other occasions with social psychology experiments (such as the Stanford Prison Experiment, conceived by psychologist Philip Zimbardo), Ron Jones' demonstration quickly began to acquire overtones of reality, and within a few days his fifteen-year old students became pawns of an oppressive system which acquired a life of its own.

The experiment

The students of Professor Jones's World History class, who were young people born after the Second World War, could not understand how it was possible the Nazis could gain so much strength in Germany, to the point they ended up causing cataclysmic global consequences.

To give his students a better understanding, Jones decided to carry out a practical demonstration, based on a series of group games.

The first day

During the first day the teacher began introducing a series of small changes in his class, typically found in dictatorships and totalitarian regimes.

The first thing he did was to increase discipline. He convinced the students of the benefits of adopting a new posture when sitting (feet touching the floor, ankles close together, legs bent 90 degrees with back straight). However, the explanations as to the benefits of this posture were just a subtle way to induce students to play along. Within just a few minutes, being correctly seated became an important issue for all of them.

Next, he established new rules in class. Among others, students should remain seated until they were give permission to leave, they would address him as Mr. Jones and any answer had to be three words or less.

With new rules having to be respected by all students, the old relationships based on popularity and dominance, typical of a teenagers' class, became invalid, and students who were previously relegated to anonymity saw their opportunity to participate in the new classroom order. Participation increased and the class became more homogeneous.

The second day

The second day, Jones focused on providing its students a sense of belonging. He wrote on the blackboard phrases such as "STRENGTH THROUGH DISCIPLINE" or "STRENGTH THROUGH COMMUNITY." After this, he organized debates around these topics and even made the whole class read the sentences aloud in unison.

Finally, he created a special salute among class members (touching the shoulder with the hand of the same arm). This gesture resembled a wave, so it was dubbed the Third Wave Salute. This salute differentiated his students from those of other classes and made them feel special.

The third day

On the third day, he assigned some students the task of ensuring the new rules were being respected and gave them the power to denounce those who broke them. He had created a fear of breaking the rules along with police to enforce them.

Students, stimulated by the practical application of knowledge, were fascinated by the experience and pressed him to continue. He was now no longer a teacher but a leader, and gradually the simulacrum of a totalitarian system he had invented began to trap the teenagers. Other students from the school asked to join the Third Wave Movement, so the teacher established a procedure for admission, in which aspiring members had to accept the rules and render obedience to the leader.

Students took it very seriously and always behaved according to the Third Wave laws.

In just three days, the experiment had turned from teacher's idea to the creation of a new reality in the school, to the point one of the students decided to be the leader's bodyguard.

Jones began to worry, and considered ending the experiment. It was not an easy decision, because the students were really fascinated with this new and practical way to assimilate knowledge, and they had a committed attitude any teacher would want from their students.

But the situation took its own course, exceeding the teacher capacity to control it. One of the students' father, who had been a prisoner of the Germans during World War II, outraged by what his son told him about the experiment, went to the school when it was empty and destroyed the classroom.

But by this time, the Third Wave Movement had spread throughout the school and had been adopted by many other students. With each passing moment, the teachers' distrust of their students increased.

The fourth day

Despite his doubts, Jones decided to continue the experiment, and on the fourth day he told his increasingly numerous students it was not a game, but they were the vanguard of a new form of government that would be implemented throughout the whole country in the coming days. All the students believed him and were willing to be an active part of the new national order.

The fifth and final day

On the last day of the experiment, Jones gathered all the students into the classroom and told them a TV program was about to announce the arrival of the Third Wave. There was a television in the classroom, so everyone waited expectantly for the statement.

Then, at the time the official announcement of the new regime arrival was supposed to take place, Professor Ron Jones abandoned his role of leader and revealed to his students the statement would not take place after all and no one would try to implement the Third Wave Order.

With care and patience, he convinced his students all had been a fiction designed to show them how easily they could be manipulated and how a totalitarian regime could seize people's will.

Curiosities

The movement's name, Third Wave, refers to the belief when the ocean waves come ashore in a series of waves, the third one is the strongest.

For a long time Ron Jones felt ashamed and remorseful about his experiment, and it was not until 1976 (nine years later) he decided to write a short story about it. After publication, the story inspired a TV series which made the events of those five days famous.

In the years following publication of his story, came more books, documentaries and even a musical. They all told how Jones managed to transform in just five days an initial group of thirty three teenagers educated in the values of democracy and freedom, into a large group of followers of a totalitarian system, which for a few moments threatened to impose a system of government on millions of people. In their minds at least.

References

Jones, R. (1976). *No Substitute for Madness! A collection of short stories by Ron Jones.* San Francisco, CA: Zephyros Educational Exchange.

DOCUMENTARY SOURCES

Hancock, M. (2010). *The Way Home*. Mark Hancock and The Wave Home. Consulted on http://www.thewavehome.com

Johnston, S. (September 5, 2008). *The Wave: the experiment that turned a school into a police state*. Londres: Telegraph Media Group Limited. Consulted on http://www.telegraph.co.uk/culture/film/3559727/The-Wave-the-experiment-that-turned-a-school-into-a-police-state.html

Jones, R. (2014). *Ron Jones. Author/Media Artist*. Ron Jones. Consulted on http://www.ronjoneswriter.com

Whiting, S. (January 30, 2010). *In 'The Wave,' ex-teacher Ron Jones looks back*. New York: SF Gate, Hearst Communications, Inc. Consulted on http://www.sfgate.com/performance/article/In-The-Wave-ex-teacher-Ron-Jones-looks-back-3274503.php

A PERSONAL EXPERIENCE: MY OWN PARTICIPATION IN A PSYCHOLOGICAL EXPERIMENT

Before concluding, I would like to briefly describe my own experience of participating in a psychological experiment when I was a college student.

During the third year of my studies, the Physiological Psychology professor requested volunteers to participate in an experiment. In return he would give the volunteers an extra point towards the final paper of his subject.

More for the reward than our contribution to science (a common attitude among participants in experiments of any kind, I am afraid) and with smiles and knowing glances, some of us volunteered to be experimental subjects.

As I recall, we were told the experiment was intended to measure the body's responses to what is known as *autogenic training*.

Autogenic training is a psychological relaxation therapy technique involving autosuggestion. Sometimes, if the degree of concentration is sufficiently high, a similar state of mind as experienced during hypnosis can be achieved.

The experiment

Before we started the experiment, our professor placed a series of electrodes and other devices throughout our bodies to measure our physiological responses. Then we all entered an experimental chamber (a confined space with room for five or six people, with thick walls and one door several centimeters thick) and the test began.

First, we heard a recording in which we were given a series of instructions on how the autogenic training session would proceed. After the instructions, the recorded voice said when the experiment was over *"we should touch our right foot with the left hand."* I made a mental note of this instruction and prepared myself, along with the rest of my smiling and excited teammates, about to enter the fascinating world of the autogenic training.

A new tape told us to focus our attention on one point in one of our hands, and slowly concentrate on that point. After several minutes, the voice told us to stretch a finger and pay attention to the stiffness feeling we would experience. Likewise, with other similar tests, I gradually moved into a state of concentration in which I only paid attention to the physical sensations indicated by the recorded voice.

Soon I lost awareness of time. The voice told us to approximate the index finger of each hand, without touching each other, and concentrate on the 'current' between them. Indeed! I felt as if they were attracted to each other, like two magnets.

The tape continued. It led us to focus on the buzz of a nonexistent fly, and I felt as if I was actually hearing it. It also told us to focus on one arm held out and rigid to the point if we tried to flex it, we would feel pain. Again to my surprise, I was almost unable to bend my arm.

So time passed, with all of us immersed in a kind of dream-state (later the teacher told us we had been into the experimental chamber for almost two hours), until the recorded voice said the experiment was over.

At that time all those present were silent, quiet and seated (except for the teacher, who was standing). I had the feeling something must be done but could not remember what.

Then I recalled my mental note about touching our right foot with the left hand. I assumed the teacher was waiting for us to do it as the test had ended, so... I bowed and touched my right foot with my left hand.

As I did so, I noticed my colleagues looked at me while smiling (with someone even openly laughing). The teacher also smiled as if something important had happened. I realized none of my fellow participants had touched their foot.

The experiment had finished.

What happened?

As we left the experimental chamber I asked why no one had touched their foot. I was told the first recording we had heard said that at the end of the experiment, as a result of the 'hypnotic' state in which we would fall, *"we would feel the uncontrollable impulse of touching our right foot with the left hand."* So that was it! My classmates and the teacher laughed because they thought I had succumbed to a deep hypnotic state, causing me to touch my foot against my will.

I guess they somehow felt superior for not having surrender to the seductive voice of the recording, then when they realized I had succumbed their belief was reinforced and perhaps made them resistant to believe me.

I tried to explain them that this was not what had happened. I told them I had touched my foot because I misunderstood the instructions, but the more I explained the more giggles, condescension and half-smiles I received. So all my efforts were in vain.

Throughout the years, while taking advantage of the friendship I had with several of them, I have tried to clarify what happened that day on several occasions. I waited slyly for the right opportunity and, pretending lack of interest, started to talk about the experiment (actually I waited impatiently and launched a planned attack) and tried to convince them of my version. As I was unable to convince them, my false lack of interest faded as I became more anxious, while trying to make them believe me.

But unfortunately my devious attempts to restore my public image were never successful. As in that now distant day of the experiment, they always answered with condescending words and turned head to hide a smile.

To this day, I still do not know what results were obtained from the experiment. I seem to remember after some weeks the teacher told us his hypothesis had been confirmed, although I do not remember what it was. The important thing for my wounded pride is I failed to convince those present that I touched my foot of my own volition, and it was a confusion when listening to the original instructions, causing me to make that move, and not a hypnotic effect.

Curiosities

Despite this small personal frustration, this experiment did arouse my interest in autogenic training.

With the help of this experience and my psychology studies I delved deeper into this technique. As a result, I came to be expert in the technique and used it for many years as an aid to falling asleep, to the point I easily fall asleep within a few minutes on those nights when, for whatever reason, it was hard for me.

At other times, I explored the concentration level I could achieve, sometimes with surprising results. Needless to say anyone interested in this technique should only practice it under the supervision of a professional.

So that was the story of my participation in a psychology experiment. On further reflection, although my failed attempts to have my side of the story believed have been a constant source of displeasure, at least it made my friends smile and gave them a good time at my expense. So perhaps this was the silver lining to my cloud.

I hope by telling my version of events I will relieve myself of this frustration of no one believing me, which I have carried for many years.

Because… you do believe me, don't you?

BIBLIOGRAPHY AND RESOURCES

BOOKS

García Vega, L. (2007). *Breve historia de la psicología.* Madrid: Siglo XXI.

Green, C. D. (2004). *Classics in the History of Psychology.* Toronto: York University. Recovered from http://psychclassics.yorku.ca/Sherif/index.htm

Real Academia Española (2014). *Diccionario de la lengua española (22ª ed.).* Consulted on http://www.rae.es

Tortosa, F. y Civera, C. (2006). *Historia de la psicología.* Madrid: McGraw Hill.

Wilde, O. (2000). *El retrato de Dorian Gray.* Madrid: Editorial Alba.

JOURNALS

American Association for the Advancement of Science, AAAS (2014). *Science.* Washington, D.C.: American Association for the Advancement of Science. Website http://www.sciencemag.org

American Psychological Association, APA (2014). *American Psychologist.* Washington, D.C.: American Psychological Association. Website http://www.apa.org/pubs/ journals/ amp

American Psychological Association, APA (2014). *History of Psychology*. Washington, D.C.: American Psychological Association. Website http://www.apa.org/pubs/ journals/ hop

American Psychological Association, APA (2014). *Journal of Abnormal and Social Psychology*. Washington, D.C.: American Psychological Association. Website http://www.apa.org/pubs/journals/abn/index.aspx

American Psychological Association, APA (2014). *Journal of Experimental Psychology*. Washington, D.C.: American Psychological Association. Website http://www.apa.org/pubs/journals/xlm/index.aspx

American Psychological Association, APA (2014). *Psychological Monographs*. Washington, D.C.: American Psychological Association. Website http://www.apa.org/pubs/databases/news/2011/11/psycarticles.aspx

American Psychological Association, APA (2014). *The Journal of General Psychology*. Washington, D.C.: American Psychological Association. Website http://www.apa.org/pubs/journals/xge

American Sociological Association (2014). *Social Psychology Quarterly*. Washington, D.C.: American Sociological Association. Website http://www.asanet.org/journals/spq/social_psychology_quarterly.cfm

American Speech-Language-Hearing Association, ASHA (1997-2014). *AJSLP*. American Journal of Speech-Language Pathology. Rockville, MD: American Speech-Language-Hearing Association. Website http://www.ajslp.pubs.asha.org

Annals of Neurosciences (2011). *Annals of Neurosciences. Official Journal of Indian Academy of Neurosciences*. Chandigarh: Annals of Neurosciences, Neuroscience Research Lab. Website

http://annalsofneurosciences.org/journal/index.php/
annal

Sussex Publishers, LLC (1991-2014). Psychology Today. New York, NY: Sussex Publishers, LLC. Website http://www.psychologytoday.com

RESOURCES

American Psychological Association, APA (2014). *APAPsycNET*. Washington, D.C.: American Psychological Association. Website http://psycnet.apa.org/ index.cfm? fa=search.defaultSearchForm

Informa UK Limited (2014). *Taylor & Francis Online. The online platform for Taylor & Francis Group content.* London: Informa UK Limited. Website http://www.tandfonline.com

ITHAKA (2000-2014). *JSTOR.* New York: ITHAKA. Website http://www.jstor.org

Noves Idees per a la Xarxa, S.L. (2013). *Proverbia.net.* Valencia: Novixar. Website http://www.proverbia.net

ABOUT ME

I was born in A Coruña (Spain) in 1973. I am a Psychology graduated from the University of Santiago de Compostela.

I began my professional career practicing in the private sector, and implementing a program for dishabituation of addictive behaviors. Later I worked as a counselor assisting young people, disadvantaged social groups and those at risk of social exclusion for job placements. In recent years I have been training people in the private sector and in collaboration with the University of A Coruña, combining these activities professionally, while writing practical psychology books.

I have been a member of the Writers' Association of Spain and part of the Author Central of Amazon for independent writers.

Please, feel free to send me your suggestions or comments. Email: ricardocalza@hotmail.es

ACKNOWLEDGMENTS

My deepest thanks to María Saavedra for her generosity, dedication and effort to review and improve the translation of this book.

ERRORS AND TYPOS

I do periodic reviews of my books to correct any mistakes I can find. If throughout the book you find any mistake, typographical error or mistranslation, please notify me by sending me an email.

I will be very grateful and I will do everything possible to correct it.